Deadly Embrace

A thriller

Eric Paice

Samuel French - London
New York - Toronto - Hollywood

ISBN 0 573 01745 X

Please see page iv for further copyright information.

DEADLY EMBRACE

First produced, under the title *Cursor* or *Deadly Embrace*, at the Mercury Theatre, Colchester, on January 23rd, 1985, with the following cast of characters:

Julia Shepherd	Anne Kidd
Liz Wolf	Lois Butlin
Steven Jones	Sion Tudor Owen
Alex Shepherd	Karen Gledhill

Directed by Michael Winter
Designed by Paul Miller
Computer Programming by Peter Dean, Jim Bowman and Thomas Nunns
Computer sound by Chris MacDonnell and Jim Bowman

Subsequently revised and produced by the Churchill Theatre, Bromley, and then toured, in 1989 with the following cast of characters:

Julia Shepherd	Hildegard Neil
Alex Shepherd	Robyn Moore
Liz Wolf	Susan Edmonstone
Steven Jones	Patrick Ryecart
Michael Shepherd	John Dough
Receptionist	Merril Dalton

Computer programmed by Gary Jones

Directed by **Nick Salmon**

CHARACTERS

Julia Shepherd: early forties, tall, slim, highly-strung
Steven Jones: thirty five, lean, good-looking, Welsh
Liz Wolf: early forties, short, vivacious, Julia's best
   friend
Alex Shepherd: eighteen, Julia's daughter, bright, a
   student
Receptionist
Michael Shepherd

ACT I
SCENE 1   Morning
SCENE 2   Late afternoon the same day
SCENE 3   That evening

ACT II
SCENE 1   Morning
SCENE 2   Two days later
SCENE 3   The following day

The action of the play takes place in Julia and Michael
Shepherd's house just outside Cambridge. Early Autumn

Time : the present

SOME SUGGESTIONS ON PRODUCTION STYLE

Although this play has a very traditional construction, it needs a fairly fluid production style. The computer, once activated, should always be threatening, both in the scene breaks and even during the interval. It is an active and apparently sensate beast that should offer menace even when it appears to be lying dormant. As the play develops, its influence should be experienced, not only by the characters onstage, but also by the audience. They should be enveloped in all round sound from the computer. It must appear to be amongst them, behind them, encompassing them. It should not be noisy or obtrusive, but quietly insistent and at times, subliminal. The voice synthesizer effect used should be persuasive and with a full range of intonation, rather than mechanical. It should be insinuating—some times sharp and reproving—and with its own sense of humour. Since the computer is described as female-friendly, it should also be sexy, not harsh or shrill. A lover's voice. It must appear to be thinking—playing with the characters on stage with subtle pauses. In brief, it is another character. Slightly distant at times, like thoughts in the mind. A voice that an audience can take home with them and that will worry them in their dreams.

The sounds the computer makes when searching for its programme, or merely watching events like a rock spider, should be anarchic, frantic, hallucinatory, as though it leads another, and far more fervent life of its own. It should also possess its own eerie halo of light to attract and ensnare the characters as they struggle to comprehend, to defy, and to escape from the genie they have released.

Eric Paice
July 1985

Special stage prop
A 640K RAM micro-computer with printer, large display screen and polyphonic sound facility.

ACT I

The Shepherds' sitting-room in a house on the outskirts of Cambridge. Morning

A chatter of electronic sound signals from a computer, like demented mice in the presence of a cat. Gradually they begin to form a recognizable tune. It is the opening bars to the "Dead March in Saul"

The Lights come up on the sitting-room. It extends right through the ground floor of the house from front to back and was formerly two rooms, now knocked together. There is a sash window at one end, with a door leading out to a quiet street. At the opposite end, french windows lead out to a secluded, but overgrown garden. One wall of the room is obscured from floor to ceiling with bookshelves from which the books, some double-stacked, are overflowing. On the opposite wall is a marble fireplace with gilt mirror decorated with gold seraphims

Although it is a spacious room, it is crowded with furniture, but none of it seems to match, as though each item had been picked up separately at a sale-room or junk shop and placed higgledy-piggledy. There are two spoonbacked chairs, more elegant than comfortable; an Edwardian sofa upholstered in raw silk, an old rolltop desk, a round table littered with bills and papers, a Victorian canterbury bursting with magazines and more papers and a jardinière containing a maidenhair fern. The marble mantelpiece carries an assortment of odd items, from pieces of fine china to old shells and fossils. The small amount of wall space left is haphazardly covered with good prints, art deco posters and a campaign poster bearing the legend "Save the Whale". The woodblock floor has a central Persian carpet and a few Peruvian scatter mats. From behind a pile of papers in the corner we shall later discover a drinks cupboard. A typical academics' room where untidiness is a sign to the world that its occupants are far too busy with intellectual pursuits to try to impress visitors with a display of order

Julia Shepherd enters from the bathroom. She carries a man's dressing-gown, hairbrush and toothbrush which she throws in the direction of a bin bag. She then goes upstairs to the gallery bedroom, which is visible to the audience, takes pyjamas from under the pillow and throws them below. Then she comes downstairs and crosses to the dining-table and proceeds to clear books and papers from the table-top into the bin bag

Julia LECHER! FORNICATOR! LYING PIG! (*Reading from a desk diary*) "Higher Education Weekend Seminar, Gosport"! Yes, well we know what he was doing that weekend ... and it had precious little to do with higher education! (*She goes to the front door as she speaks, opens it and throws the bin bag out. She slams the door and crosses to the dining-table*) Gosport ... !

Alex enters from the archway UR. *She carries a weekend bag. She tosses the bag on the chair above the coffee table and crosses into the kitchen*

Alex Having a little clear out, Mother?
Julia (*turning to see her, trying to control her temper*) Oh, no darling, I'm just spring-cleaning ...
Alex In October?
Julia Alex, are you rushing back to college straight away?
Alex Yes, I've got three hours of Freud this morning. Why?
Julia Well, there's something rather serious that we have to talk about ...
Alex Like Daddy getting the boot?
Julia You ... heard ...
Alex I imagine they heard you in John o' Groats! You two have been at it since three o'clock this morning.
Julia I'm terribly sorry about all this.
Alex I don't really think you're sorry at all. I think you're furious.
Julia I meant sorry it's happened and particularly sorry for you.
Alex Why me?
Julia Well, it's bound to be a bit of a shock to wake up one morning to find that you belong to a one-parent family.
Alex Mother, I'm eighteen! What on earth difference is it going to make to me now? Besides, most of my friends come from broken homes. As a matter of fact, I was starting to feel a bit of a freak.
Julia Oh God ...
Alex Anyway, I take it I'm still going to see Daddy from time to time. I assume he's not disappearing off the face of the earth.
Julia Of course not darling ... I've got to talk to you about all this ...
Alex Look, I really must go or I'll miss my train.
Julia When will I see you again?
Alex I'm back at the weekend. I'll call you. Try and relax, Mother, or you'll just end up with one of your migraines. Pop a pill.
Julia A pill, what a good idea ...

Liz knocks at the front door and comes in

Liz Can I come in?
Alex (*seeing Liz*) Here comes the cavalry! (*She goes to collect a couple of books from a pile, so delaying her exit*)

Liz is smartly dressed, bouncy, excited at the prospect of a good gossip. She is holding the pyjama trousers between two fingers

Liz Julia darling, what are you doing? A perfectly good pair of silk pyjamas. They could go to Oxfam. Help the Third World.
Julia What the hell does the Third World want with silk pyjamas?
Liz They're not fussy. They probably made them in the first place.

She sees Alex, trying to slip quietly away, and turns on her in massive sympathy

Oh Alex, you poor child. You must be totally devastated!

Alex Must I?

Liz Oh dear ... (*To Julia*) Does she know?

Julia Yes, she's just putting a brave face on it ...

Alex (*firmly*) 'Bye everyone, have fun!

She exits rapidly, slamming the door after her

Liz immediately turns her attention back to Julia, ready to take over command of the emotional crisis

Liz Now Julia darling, I want you to calm down and tell me all about it.

Julia I'm perfectly calm now, thank you, Liz. (*Suddenly*) Look at this! (*She has found a credit card statement, which she now reads out to Liz, her anger rising again as she does so*) "La Strada Restaurant. Seventy-six pounds, fifty." What the hell was she eating, the greedy cow?

Liz You should have checked his American Express statement before, dear. It's a bit late now.

Julia (*reading from another entry*) "Inter-Continental Hotel Geneva" ... That was the weekend he was supposed to be in Cardiff ...

Liz No use crying over spilt champagne, darling.

Julia For the past six months he has pretended that he was impotent!

Liz So? What are you missing. Anyway, that's the oldest trick in the tom-cat's manual. Now just relax, Julia. The way you're going on, anyone would think it was your lover. And it could all work out for the best. The gods of adultery move in mysterious ways, their wonders to perform. So just calm yourself down ...

Julia I'm perfectly calm, Liz.

Liz No you're not. You're all hyped up and tense. I can feel it. Now just sit down and take thirty seconds' meditation while I get you a drink. (*She steers Julia over to a spoonback chair and seats her*) Now where do you keep your vodka?

Julia Over there, behind a pile of CND minutes. Thank you for coming round so quickly, Liz.

Liz Darling, this is an emergency! The moment I got your call, I dropped everything, leapt into the Renault and drove over Magdalene Bridge like a maniac, scattering a whole flock of Spanish language students on pink bicycles. It was like ploughing through flamingoes. (*She starts to pour the vodka liberally into two glasses*)

Julia Water with mine, love. Half and half.

Liz Oh, sod the water. You gulp it down neat, girl. (*She comes back with the two glasses, hands one to Julia*) Right. Now you must tell me all the gory details. Chin-chin!

Julia I thought I was supposed to be meditating.

Liz Then do it out aloud.

Julia I'm not really sure I feel like talking about it at the moment.

Liz But of course you do, darling. That's why you rang me. What else are best friends for?

Julia Well, he's gone off. What else is there to say?

Liz Darling, the first thing you have to realize is that this is a very common experience. Husbands are going off all over Cambridge. It's something to do with the long hot summer.

Julia But after fourteen years, Liz. I mean one is entitled to regard one's husband as a permanent fixture. Like the kitchen cupboards.

Liz I know, darling. And you've been very smug about it. But now you're one of us. Thank God. (*She settles down for a cosy gossip*) Who's he gone off with. Anyone we know?

Julia No, sorry to disappoint you, Liz.

Liz Are you sure? I know all the itchy wives from here to Granchester.

Julia I don't really know for certain. He's being deliberately vague about the bitch.

Liz Oh, that's disgraceful. Going off with another woman is bad enough, but not telling you who it is amounts to mental cruelty. How did you find out?

Julia She sent him a revolting birthday card which he was stupid enough to leave where I was absolutely bound to find it.

Liz Where?

Julia In his briefcase.

Liz (*laughing*) Was it signed?

Julia "From your darling Cuddles."

Liz (*bursting into a peal of laughter*) Cuddles! I don't believe it. I mean for a lecturer in Economics and Political Science. Cuddles! No wonder the country's in a mess. Didn't you once have a cat called Cuddles?

Julia I don't think it's particularly funny, Liz.

Liz (*giggling*) Of course not darling, I'm very sorry. Did you check the postmark?

Julia No.

Liz Oh, you should always check the postmark. So, where is he at the moment?

Julia I don't know. I just threw him out, neck and crop. He's probably gone to a hotel.

Liz This is beginning to sound rather serious, darling.

Julia Well of course it's serious! The marriage is finished. Over. He made that perfectly clear.

Liz Right. So what are you going to plan to do now? Divorce him?

Julia Not bloody likely! Let him sweat for the rest of his life.

Liz That's my girl. You're starting to sound like an abandoned wife already.

Julia The way I feel now, I'd like to kill the bastard.

Liz Perfectly normal reaction, darling. When mine walked out five years ago, I felt like bashing him on the bald patch with a steam iron. At least I'd have got the insurance money. The only snag is, you get caught. Then for some absurd reason they refuse to pay out.

Julia Pity there's no way of doing it without getting caught.

Pause

Liz Speaking of money, as one must at times of deep emotional stress, chin-chin, has he made any provision for you?

Julia He muttered something about an allowance, but he'll never keep that up. He's insured up to the hilt of course, but that's no use to me while he's alive.

Liz What do you call "up to the hilt"?

Julia If he dies, I get the equivalent of his annual salary up to his retirement age—as he's got about fifteen years to go, it amounts to a quarter of a million quid.

Liz A quarter of a million? You never told me Michael was worth all that, Julia?

Julia Only when he's dead. He's not worth a light while he's still alive.

Liz Then you never know. I mean he's got a dicky heart, hasn't he? And with a brand new mistress, he's bound to try and prove he's sexually athletic. Men of that age always do. Then . . . bingo. He dies on the job. Cuddles could prove a blessing in disguise, darling.

Julia (*drily*) He tells me it's an intellectual relationship.

Liz Oh, come on. You've lived in Cambridge long enough to know that intellectuals go at it like bloody rabbits, except when they're married of course!

Julia That was not the most thoughtful remark, Liz.

Liz Oh, I'm sorry. I was just trying to look on the bright side.

Julia There isn't a bright side. I feel betrayed, insulted and degraded. (*She takes out a handkerchief and starts to sniffle*)

Liz comes over and puts an arm round her

Liz Now you mustn't upset yourself. He's not worth wasting any tears over. It's too late for remorse now, anyway.

Julia It's not remorse. It's bloody fury.

Liz Oh, that's all right then. Have another vodka.

Julia I really don't think I should, Liz. I've already taken a chlorpromazine. Alcohol will just make me sleepy.

Liz goes over to top up her glass

Liz A nice sleep'll do you good. And when you wake up, you'll suddenly realize you're free. Free to do anything you want without ever having to explain it to anyone!

Julia Such as?

Liz (*casting around for an example*) Well . . . you can read in bed for as long as you want with the light on.

Julia Big deal.

Liz Or . . . start a career.

Julia I'm not trained for anything. All I am is a bloody housewife.

Liz All right then, take a lover. Take two if you feel up to it. I've always said that women of our age need at least two lovers.

Julia (*cheering up a bit, smiling*) Why two?

Liz One for bed. The other to put up bookshelves.

Julia Can't one perform both functions?

Liz I never met one that could. Just think, darling, tomorrow you could meet a young, tall, dark, handsome millionaire.

Julia In Cambridge?

Liz Stranger things have happened. And in the meantime, just grab the first man that walks through that door.

Julia With my luck it'll be a Jehovah's Witness.

Liz So. At least you'll survive the holocaust. Oooh listen darling, I must go. I've got to be at Heathrow by midday. Boring trip to Paris to look at some schmutter. I'll send you a postcard from the Louvre. Something taste-ful—like a statue with a big stone dong.

Julia Gee, thanks Liz.

Liz You feeling better now?

Julia A bit. Thanks for coming round.

Liz collects her handbag, kisses Julia on the cheek and goes to exit

Liz Call on me any time you're feeling low. And don't forget what I said. You're free now, Julia. Your marriage is over. It's like coming out of gaol. At first you blink at the light and can't believe you're free. But you are. The world is now your oyster, darling. 'Bye.

She goes out waving

Julia (*partly to Liz, partly to herself*) I don't want a bloody oyster, I just want to kill the bastard!

The Lights fade to Black-out

SCENE 2

The same. Afternoon

The light is now fading. Julia is sitting in the rocking-chair, her feet up on the footstool, asleep

The sound of a van approaching and pulling up outside on the gravel. We hear the engine turned off and the door slam. Steven Jones appears at the open front door. He carries a large cardboard box and briefcase

Steven Good-afternoon. (*He enters and moves slowly* DS *of the pillar having some difficulty with his load*) Good-afternoon!

This time Julia stirs, half-awake. She sits up

I hope I'm not disturbing you. Do you mind if I come in?

Julia You seem to be in already.

Steven sets his box and briefcase down on the floor. He kneels and begins to extract his clipboard from his briefcase. Pause

Steven Hallo ...

Julia Can I help you?

Julia is now fully awake and takes a good look at him. She likes what she sees. Steven stands up looking through the notes on his clipboard

Steven Someone in this house should have a sixteen-K Minibrain with dual floppy attachments.

Julia That sounds just like my husband. He isn't here at the moment. Who are you?

Steven Jones, madam, Steven Jones of Steven Jones Software Great Britain Incorporated, plc. (*He proffers a business card*) Managing Director, Executive Director and High-Technology Specialist.

Julia Oh, I see, a salesman. What are you selling?

Steven Software.

Julia Nighties? Flannel knickers?

Steven Pardon?

Julia Software.

Steven Computer software, I've come to update your husband's equipment.

Julia Yes, well, you're a little late for that. He's gone.

Steven Oh dear, I wish I'd known.

Julia (*icily*) Yes, so do I.

Steven (*putting down his equipment*) Well, it'll be a nice surprise for him when he gets back. Do you happen to have his Minibrain to hand?

Julia crosses to the corner, shifts a pile of papers and emerges with a small home computer keyboard

Julia Do you mean that old thing? I was about to throw it out.

Steven Oh no! Don't do that! I'll tell you what I'll do. I'll offer you twice the price he paid for it in part exchange for the brand new six hundred and forty-K Aladdin Genie. (*He unclips his large case and takes out a much larger computer with more elaborate keyboard*)

Julia New computers for old?

Steven With a slight adjustment, of course, but we can do that on a leasing arrangement, so initially it'll actually cost less. Where is your nearest power source?

Julia Gas or electric?

Steven Electric, madam. Computers don't run on gas.

Julia Follow the Hoover lead.

Steven Ah, yes ...

Steven has already set up the keyboard on the desk, now gets down on the floor to move aside a pile of papers to reveal a double point. He plugs it in. Julia watches him for a moment

Julia But there really isn't much point, Mr Jones. My husband is likely to be away for a very long time, and I have absolutely no use for a computer.

Steven Ah, but I have to prove it's in working order, you don't want to buy a pig in a poke. (*He gets to his feet again*) Besides, you may find it a great comfort while he's away.

Julia Oh, really, how?

Steven Oh, you can play space games or noughts and crosses. Now, if you're not too familiar with computer hardware, this is the basic unit, the keyboard. (*He opens the second case and takes out what looks like a small television monitor*) This is what we call the Visual Display Unit or VDU and the third basic item is what we high technology people call the printer P.R.I.N.T.E.R.

Julia I can spell printer, Mr Jones.

Steven Oh, well then you're half-way there already. Right. So much for the basic hardware. (*He takes up a lecturer's pose, walking up and down*) Now what, I hear you ask, do we mean by software?

Julia You didn't, but I'm sure you're going to tell me.

Steven Software, Mrs Shepherd, is divided into two basic categories. The operating systems stored in the memory of the micro-processor itself (*tapping the keyboard by way of illustration*), and the program they operate, or as we call it, the menu. (*He takes two discs out of his briefcase, a five-inch floppy disc and an eight-inch hard disc*) M.E.N.U.

Julia I can also spell menu.

Steven Oh good, then you'll have no problem with computer language. Now the program or menu is stored either on a five-inch floppy, or an eight-inch hard.

Julia What's the difference?

Steven The eight-inch hard has a greater duration.

Julia But of course, silly me.

Steven Are you following me so far, madam?

Julia With rapt attention, Mr Jones.

Steven Right, now why, you may ask, do we need two kinds of software, and the answer is amazingly simple. The role of the former is to tell the latter what to do.

Julia The five-inch floppy tells the eight-inch hard.

Steven (*patiently*) No, the operating system tells the external program or applications software.

Julia Of course. I should have known!

Steven Now the Aladdin Genie has a storage capacity of six hundred and forty kilobytes.

Julia Kilo whats?

Steven No, kilobytes. A kilobyte is made up of one thousand and twenty-four bytes and each byte is made of eight bits.

Julia Gosh.

Steven So, for convenience, we refer to the total capacity six forty K RAM.

Julia Ram?

Steven R.A.M.

Julia A male sheep or stud.

Steven No. RAM means Random-Access Memory. There's also ROM, PROM and EPROM, but I don't want to confuse the issue.

Julia Oh, no, let's stick with the ram. That sounds like much more fun.

Steven There are two kinds of RAM. Static and dynamic.

Julia I'll take the dynamic.

Steven Pardon?

Julia Is he the one that gives you a thousand and twenty-four bites?

Steven (*after a fraction's pause*) I don't think you're quite basically following me.

Julia No, but never mind, Mr Jones, it's all deliciously vulgar.

Steven (*hurt*) No, there is nothing vulgar about computer software Mrs Shepherd. It's all extremely refined.

Julia I'm sure it is, I'm so sorry, please carry on.

Steven Yes ... um ... I seem to have ... er ... basically lost my train of thought for the moment.

Julia Mr Jones, were you ever by any chance, a polytechnic lecturer?

Steven Oh, well, that's very perceptive of you. How did you know?

Julia You keep using the word "basically". You also walk up and down with your hands behind your back addressing your feet.

Steven (*stopping immediately*) Oh yes ... I hadn't noticed.

Julia Would you like a glass of water?

Steven Oh, yes, that would be very kind of you.

Julia Where were you lecturing?

Steven South East London Poly. Computer Science and basic programming ... I mean, fundamental programming.

Julia Anything with the water?

Steven (*hopefully*) Like ... what?

Julia Drop of vodka to take away the taste?

Steven Oh, well, I shouldn't really, I'm driving, see ... but since you offered ...

Julia You'll change your mind. (*She tops up the glass with vodka, then her own*)

Steven Well, anyway, when the market opened up for personal computers, I remembered the words of our Prime Minister. "Now is the time", she said, "to help create a new Britain."

Julia (*coming over to him with the drinks*) And what happened then?

Steven I was made redundant. (*Taking the glass*) Thank you. But I knew this was my chance to start up my own business and make myself a fortune.

Julia And have you made yourself a fortune, Mr Jones?

Steven Well ... not quite yet, but within three years I fully expect to have made my first million.

Julia (*raising her glass*) Well, cheers, Mr Jones. Here's to the first million.

Steven Thank you very much. Your very good health, Mrs Shepherd. Now, if you'll just key your name in Aladdin, we can start the demonstration.

Julia Mr Jones, my husband may very well have ordered this machine, but he certainly isn't going to be here to use it.

Steven (*slowly*) Oh, you mean ... he's not coming back?

Julia You're very quick on the uptake, Mr Jones.

Steven gives her a quick glance which she meets steadily

Steven Ah ... in that case, may I introduce you to my special program for abandoned wives. (*He takes out a package of floppy discs from his*

briefcase and puts one of them into the memory box slot) Now, just type in
your name and press "enter", and you will be truly amazed.

*Julia keys in her name. The computer starts a mad squeaking noise which
forms itself into a recognizable tune to the words of:*

Aladdin   Good-morning, good-morning
                     It's great to be up late,
                     Good-morning, good-morning ... to you.
Good-morning Mrs Julia Shepherd, you are looking inexpressibly beautiful today, if I may say so. I am the Aladdin Genie and I can grant you
three wishes. May I come into your life?

Julia It speaks!

Steven They'll soon be making ones that walk.

Aladdin Your wish is my command, Julia Shepherd, we could have fun
together.

Steven Pretty sexy eh?

Julia It depends what turns you on.

Steven Well, yes, but what do you think of it as a sales technique?

*Julia puts two fingers delicately to her nose and with the other hand mimes the
pulling of a chain*

(*Disappointed*) Oh dear. It worked like a charm in Luton.

Julia How many inexpressibly beautiful Mrs Julia Shepherds did you find
in Luton, Mr Jones?

Steven The names are interchangeable. The moment the prospective customer keys her own name in, Aladdin erases the previous one and
updates. Like ... "Good-morning Mrs Maisie Murgatroyd, you're
looking very ..."—you know, however she's looking ...

Julia Good-morning Mrs Julia Shepherd, you're looking inexpressibly
intellectual today, honeypot.

Steven (*continuing to put together the computer components*) Yes, yes,
something on those lines.

Julia Mr Jones, before you get too engrossed in your work, may I say once
and for all, I have absolutely no use for a computer. I have nothing to
compute.

Steven (*with a bit of a patronizing smile*) Women always react that way at
the outset. That's because all previous software programs have been
male-orientated. Mine is female-orientated, or as we say in the trade,
female-friendly.

Julia All right, Mr Jones. I have tried. Carry on ...

Steven holds up the first of the three floppy discs

Steven Allow me to introduce ... HOUSEMAN.

Julia Houseman?

Steven It's an acronym: Home Operations Using Servile Male Assistant
Nodules. No housewife should be without one.

Julia But what does it actually do?

Steven Anything you want. All you have to do is insert the five-inch floppy into the top slot. (*He removes the sales promotion disc and inserts the next disc*)

Julia And what do you put in the bottom slot?

Steven That one's for the eight-inch hard ... and now it's ready to serve you. Now, what would you like more than anything in the world at the moment? Just close your eyes and think ...

Julia (*closing her eyes*) Four weeks in the Caribbean?

Steven No problem. (*He goes to his capacious box*) All we need is a modem.

Julia A what?

Steven A modulator/demodulator. Sometimes known as an acoustic coupler ... (*He produces a modem—a square box with a cradle to take a telephone receiver and buttons for dialling*) Or, to the layman, a telephone attachment. (*He places it beside her telephone, takes the telephone receiver off its own cradle and places it on the modem cradle*)

Julia Aladdin can use the telephone?

Steven Only to other computers, of course. And providing they're compatible. But given that, he can chat away for hours.

Julia I've got a daughter like that.

Steven Oh, really? Well, all we do now is to call up the computer terminal of any major airline or tour operator ... and in a matter of seconds it will book your flight, make your hotel reservation and even tell you the local sea temperature. (*He moves over to the keyboard to start to play*)

Julia Mr Jones, does he also pay the fare?

Steven He can charge it to your credit card—

Julia Thank you very much, Mr Jones ... forget it!

Steven (*disappointed*) Oh. How about shopping?

Julia Aladdin can do my shopping for me?

Steven He can make a complete program of everything in your food cupboard, along with your average rate of usage. He can then tell you exactly when, say, the tomato ketchup's running low and instruct you to re-order.

Julia But I can see that, Mr Jones, by looking at the bottle.

Steven Yes, well ... this saves you the bother. Then take the household cleaning—Aladdin can give you a definite checklist of everything to be done at regular intervals, from changing the sheets to ... (*Looking around for an example*) Tidying the bookshelves.

Julia May I ask you a personal question?

Steven Yes, by all means.

Julia Are you married?

Steven Er ... not at the moment, my wife left me last Christmas.

Julia Were you surprised?

Steven I was extremely puzzled. Do you know I'd succeeded in reducing her housework out-put to one hour a day. And do you know what she did with the time I'd saved her?

Julia Took a lover?

Steven The carpet-cleaning man.

Julia Life is like that, Mr Jones.

Steven Well, when my wife went off with the carpet-cleaning man, I suddenly had this brilliant idea of a new female-friendly program. (*He holds up the disc triumphantly*) AFFAIR!

Julia Another acronym?

Steven Anonymous Fun Factor At Imminent Risk.

Julia Why imminent risk?

Steven My researches indicate that most women conducting an affair like to feel they might just be found out. It adds a certain spice to the infidelity. Take my wife, for example, she was always spilling things on the carpet.

Julia Perhaps she wanted you to buy her a new one, Mr Jones.

Steven Oh, well, I hadn't thought of that ... The AFFAIR menu arranges times and places for the guilty parties to meet. It has ample storage for illicit love letters translated into binary code and security-locked with your own personal key code. The package comes complete with a range of diversionary response data to confuse suspicious husbands. I call that ALIBI.

Julia A Load of Improbable Bullshit?

Steven You're getting very good at computer acronyms, Mrs Shepherd. You have a creative mind.

Julia Mr Jones, how well did you know my husband?

Steven Ah, well, would you like me to be completely frank?

Julia Why not?

Steven I never met him in my life.

Julia I thought not. So he didn't buy a sixteen-K Minibrain from you?

Steven I didn't actually say it was from me. You see, what happened was this. The Minibrain dealers went broke so I managed to acquire their customer list from a friend who worked for them. (*Vaguely*) There was a contract to update the equipment, so I thought I should shoulder that responsibility.

Julia And once you'd got your foot in the door, try to flog the wife your software.

Steven (*with a smile*) If you're going to be a millionaire, Mrs Shepherd, you have to show a bit of enterprise.

Julia Another glass of water?

Steven Oh, I shouldn't really. I'm driving, see ...

Julia Couldn't Aladdin do that for you?

Steven No, he keeps failing his driving test on the hill start.

Julia helps herself to the vodka bottle, Steven watches her for a moment, then:

I suppose I ... could sleep in my van for the night. Unless of course you know of a bed and breakfast handy?

Julia I might. (*And leaves it hanging in the air*)

Steven I ... er ... forgot to mention. Anyone interested in the Aladdin Genie gets seven days' personal instruction thrown in. It's what we call the Hands-on Experience.

Julia You made that one up, Mr Jones.

They are now close together again

Steven No, honestly, it's a ... genuine computer buzzword ...

And in a moment they are in a tight clinch. The Lights begin to fade. Steven finally comes up for air

(*Jubilantly*) Does that mean I've made a sale, Mrs Shepherd?
Julia Seven days' trial, with no obligation to purchase.
Steven No, no, no. No obligation at all, Mrs Shepherd.

They kiss again

Julia Shall we go upstairs?
Steven It's only six-thirty, I don't think I'm feeling very sleepy.
Julia That's good.

They move up the stairs towards the gallery bedroom

Alex enters by the front door, stops on hearing their voices and remains underneath the gallery floor listening. She notices the computer boxes

Shouldn't we turn that thing off?
Steven As far as power consumption goes, Aladdin is basically very economical.
Julia Basically?
Steven Yes ... I keep using that word ...

The both laugh

Anyway, he promised he wouldn't peep. (*He removes her cardigan*) You're a very beautiful woman Mrs Shepherd.
Julia My name is Julia, Mr Jones.
Steven Ah ... yes, Julia.

They settle on the bed as the Lights fade to Black-out

SCENE 3

The same. Later that evening

Julia is alone in bed. She wakes up and sits up

Julia Steven? Where are you? Steven? (*She switches on the bedside lamp*) Oh well, easy come ... I thought he might at least have stayed the night.

Steven enters the front door, barefoot in trousers and shirt. He carries a holdall. He switches on the main lights

Steven ... ? (*She comes downstairs*)
Steven Oh, hallo lovely.
Julia Where have you been?
Steven Oh, just out to the van. You'd fallen asleep. You were looking so beautiful.
Julia There's no need to keep up the sales patter.

Steven No, no, I really mean it. I'm just crazy about older women.

Julia (*looking at the holdall*) What have you got there?

Steven (*holding up the contents*) Nothing much. Pair of knickers and a toothbrush.

Julia I see. So you came prepared to stay, just in case. You should have told me, I needn't have wasted all that vodka.

Steven Oh, no, it's just that I keep everything in my van, see.

Julia I thought you had a home in Luton.

Steven No, that went to the wife . . . and the carpet-cleaning man.

Julia Where is your office?

Steven (*with a self-deprecating smile*) Also in my van. At the moment.

Julia What about your staff? Are they in the van too?

Steven Staff?

Julia You haven't got any staff?

Steven No, not at the moment.

Julia I thought you said you were the Managing Director of Steven Jones Software plc something-or-other, incorporated . . .

Steven It's one of the more attractive aspects of Company Law that to be a Managing Director, you don't have to have anyone either to manage or direct.

Julia In other words, Steven Jones, you are a homeless bum.

Steven I'm a high-technology homeless bum.

Julia Do you even own Aladdin?

Steven Technically speaking, the bank owns Aladdin. But I have put down the first payment.

Julia On your credit card?

Steven Oh all right, so I'm a high-technology homeless bum trying to make his first sale.

Julia You're also a bit of a liar, aren't you?

Steven No. I never tell lies. I might lead people away from the truth occasionally, but I can't help that. I'm Welsh. Look if you're really going to throw me out now, do you mind if I have a shower first?

Julia (*kissing him*) I'm not throwing you out, Steven. I have a soft spot for the poor, the homeless and the dispossessed. It's just a pity you're not from the Third World.

Steven I am. Wales is a Third-World country. That's why I left.

Julia Go and have your shower.

Steven (*going to exit*) As soon as I get back, we start on the first lesson, so go and warm up the keyboard.

Julia I was going to get dinner.

Steven Work before pleasure, my sweet.

He exits to the bathroom

Julia (*looking at the computer*) What do I do?

Steven (*off*) Type in "Hallo" and press "enter".

We hear the shower, off

Julia (*speaking as she types*) H.A.L.L.O. Enter. (*She presses a button*)

Aladdin makes a squeaking sound and plays the tune "Good-morning, good-morning" then:

Aladdin Hallo Penny, how are you today?
Julia I'm not Penny. (*She types*)
Aladdin Hallo Pamela, how are you today?
Julia (*as she types*) I'm Julia!
Aladdin Hallo, Juliet. You are looking inexpressibly beautiful today.
Julia I thought you fancied me, you idiot machine!

The telephone rings

Aladdin Hallo Margaret.
Julia Hang on!
Aladdin Hallo Cynthia.

Julia picks up the receiver

    Hallo Janice.
Julia Oh, shut up! (*Into the phone*) Sorry, not you. . . . Oh, hallo Liz . . .
Aladdin Hallo Liz.
Julia Sweet of you to call.
Aladdin Hallo Jemimah, Hallo Doreen. Hallo Rosalind. Hallo Sally. Hallo Cathy . . .
Julia Just a minute, Liz. I've got a mad parrot here. (*She calls off*) How do you stop this thing?
Steven (*off; calling from the bathroom*) Press "exit".

The shower stops. Julia presses the button

Aladdin Hallo——(*A squeak as the button is pressed*)
Julia (*into the phone*) Sorry Liz. So where are you? . . . Champs-Elysées. What fun. Have you found someone to share your bidet yet? . . . Well, happy hunting. Me? . . . Oh, I'm feeling a lot better this evening. . . . Mind your own business. But I tell you what I have acquired. A promiscuous computer. . . . How should I know? I haven't looked underneath. Male I imagine, the way it's going through its little black book.

Steven enters from the bathroom wearing Julia's pink towelling dressing-gown

    Listen, darling, I must go. The plumber's just arrived. . . . The twenty-four-hour type. Have a lovely time. See you when you get back. 'Bye darling. (*She hangs up*)
Steven Who's "darling"? I'm jealous.
Julia My old friend Liz. You'd like her, she's fun.
Steven Just as long as she's old. What's the problem with Aladdin?
Julia He doesn't seem to know me any more.
Steven Ah. That's because your name is still in the limbo file. You were only a prospective buyer then, see. Now you're an established owner I can transfer you into the directory. Here we go. (*He keys in her name*) Now, try again.

Julia types

Aladdin Hallo Julia, how are you today?
Steven There. Clever, eh?
Julia But who were all those other women?
Steven What other women?
Julia Penny, Pamela, Juliet, Janice, Jemimah . . .
Steven Sounds like garbage to me.
Julia Garbage?
Steven Someone playing around, entered them into the directory and forgot
   about them.
Julia Who?
Steven Well, I don't know. Previous owner maybe.
Julia I thought it was new.
Steven Er, yes, well, I have to admit, I, er bought it at an auction.
Julia So you were trying to fob me off with a second-hand machine?
Steven No, you'd get a new one direct from the manufacturers. Now come
   on. Let's get back to the lesson.
Julia How?
Steven Press "run".
Aladdin Would you like to play a game, Julia?
Julia (*to Steven*) What kind of game?
Steven Don't know. Shouldn't be any games in the memory.
Julia So what do I do?
Steven Just type "Y" for "yes". I'm as mystified as you are.

Julia keys in

Aladdin Which game?
Steven Ask it what games it's got. Press control key and "L" for listing.
Julia (*keying in*) Control and "L".
Aladdin One: The Money Game. Two: The Crossword Game. Three: The
   Murder Game.
Julia } (*together*) What's that?
Aladdin } Four: The Submarine Game.
Steven } (*together*) Haven't a clue . . .
Aladdin } Five: The Racing Game.
Julia Let's play that one . . .
Steven All right. Press three.

*Julia keys in. Aladdin suddenly starts to play the first few bars of the "Dead
March in Saul" in its little mouse squeak tones, then:*

Aladdin (*in sepulchral tones*) MURDER!
Steven Charming. Do you want to give it a go?
Julia Why not?
Steven Press "enter".
Aladdin Who do you wish to murder, Julia?
Steven Up to you, lovely.
Julia All right. Let's say "X".

Steven Press "enter" ...
Aladdin Age of "X"?
Julia Fifty-three. (*She keys in*)
Aladdin Sex?
Julia (*keying in*) Male.
Aladdin Motive? Select from: One: money. Two: jealousy. Three: revenge.

Julia hesitates for a moment, then:

Julia Can I pass?
Steven No. No passing allowed.
Julia (*keying in*) Revenge.
Aladdin Select murder weapon. One: blunt instrument. Two: sharp instrument. Three: poison. Four: strangulation. Five: firearms. Six: computer choice.
Julia (*keying in*) Strangulation.
Aladdin Invalid choice.
Julia (*to Steven*) Why?
Steven I don't know. Press question mark.
Julia (*keying in*) Why?
Aladdin Female physical inadequacy.
Steven Sexist beast!
Julia (*keying in*) Computer to choose.
Aladdin Poison. Body Disposal. Select. One: burial. Two: cremation. Three: dissolution in acid.
Steven Now there's a quaint old English custom.
Aladdin Four: dismemberment and dispersal.
Steven You'd need a blinking helicopter!
Aladdin Five: compost heap. Six: computer choice.
Julia Five: compost heap.
Aladdin Invalid choice.
Julia (*keying in*) Why?
Aladdin Poison traces in soil.
Steven Then along comes PC Prodnose. "I see your climbers are wilting a bit, Mrs Shepherd. Have you been up to mischief?"
Aladdin I can do better. To remove poison traces select Two: cremation.
Julia But if there's been a murder, there'll be an autopsy before the body goes for cremation.
Steven Autopsy, question mark and enter.
Julia (*keying in*) Autopsy. Enter.
Aladdin Verdict. Accidental overdose. Select poison. One: arsenic. Two: strychnine. Three: mercury. Four: prussic acid. Five: digitalis. Six: computer choice.
Julia (*keying in*) One: arsenic.
Aladdin Invalid choice. Can you do better?

There is a fraction's pause. Julia does not move, but sits by the keyboard frozen for a moment

Steven Well, go on. Show that smart-arse.

Julia I know what it wants me to choose. (*She keys in*) Five: digitalis?

Aladdin Correct. Go to seven hundred.

Julia (*suddenly in alarm*) Switch that damn thing off!

Steven Why, what's wrong?

Julia Just stop it, Steven!

Steven All right. Simple. (*He keys in*)

Aladdin Escape. Escape. Escape.

Steven What's the matter?

Julia I know you're going to think I'm paranoid, but I believe that computer is reading my mind.

Steven That's impossible. Micro-processors aren't telepathic.

Julia It knows what I really want!

Steven That's just crazy.

Julia When it asked me how I wanted to kill him, what I really wanted to say was poison. I chose something else deliberately. It rejected that and came back to poison.

Steven OK, so maybe most women think of poison when they think of murder.

Julia How would it know I'm a woman?

Steven I told you. Aladdin is female-friendly.

Julia I want a serious answer, Steven.

Steven You keyed in your name earlier, maybe it stored that piece of information . . . or maybe when you gave the sex of the victim as male, it assumed you were female. How should I know?

Julia When it asked how I wanted to get rid of the body, my first choice was cremation. It rejected any other choice.

Steven It also said that it was a logical choice . . .

Julia And, again with the kind of poison. What I wanted to say was digitalis. I tried saying arsenic, but it wouldn't have it.

Steven So, what are you trying to say?

Julia Ever since my husband walked out on me, I've wanted to kill him. By amazing coincidence, you walk through the door with a murder program: or was it a coincidence?

Steven How could I possibly know your husband had even left you, let alone that you wanted to wipe him out?

Julia Someone could have put you up to it. Whoever put that program in there in the first place. You could be working together. All that sales bullshit was just you worming your way into my confidence.

Steven Let me remind you that it was *you* who seduced *me*, not the other way round. Maybe *I'm* the one who's being taken for a ride!

Julia How?

Steven I don't know. You're the one who's throwing suspicion around. As far as I'm concerned, this is just a crazy computer game. If it happens to fit in with some deep subliminal desire of yours, how am I to know. Uh? Jesus, women are so infuriating. They don't understand technology, so they have to turn the whole thing into a mystic experience! Look, let's forget the whole thing and play a nice harmless game of intergalactic warfare.

Julia No, no. Let's go on with this one. (*She crosses back to the keyboard*)
Steven (*exasperated*) So what was the big scene about?
Julia I just wanted to make sure you weren't stringing me along.
Steven And are you sure now?
Julia (*not offensively*) Yes, I don't really think you're bright enough. How do I get the game back again?
Steven Well, carry on from where you left off. What was the last command?
Julia Go to seven hundred.
Steven Right. Key that in.
Julia (*keying in*) Go to seven hundred.
Aladdin Murder menu. Resume. Victim X. Sex male. Age fifty-three. Motive revenge. Murder weapon poison. Type of poison digitalis. Body disposal cremation. Please identify X.
Julia (*keying in*) Why?
Aladdin I cannot proceed without the identity of X.

Steven looks at Julia, she pauses for a moment, then keys in

Julia Michael John Shepherd.
Aladdin Name hospital where medical records are kept.
Julia Mid-Anglia General.
Aladdin Good.
Julia Why?
Aladdin Computer compatible. I can obtain access.
Julia (*to Steven*) Is that possible?
Steven No. Clinical records would be heavily code-locked. I think it's bluffing.
Aladdin Name consultant.
Julia Mr Jonathan Grey.
Aladdin Wait please.
Julia What's it doing now?
Steven Scanning its memory bank.
Aladdin I have PEC.
Steven Personal Entry Code. That would be Grey's own code to obtain access to the computer.
Julia How would it get that?
Steven Haven't a clue ...
Aladdin C R A C Code two seven seven eight Cromwell SX-one.

Julia looks to Steven for an explanation

Steven Clinical Records Access Code ...
Julia I thought you said it was bluffing.
Aladdin Attach modem.

Steven crosses to the telephone, picks up the receiver and places it on the modem

Wait please.

A dialling sound is heard

Julia What's it doing now?

Steven Dialling straight through to the Mid-Anglia computer.

Julia Where did it get the telephone number from?

Steven Scanned the directory. That's the least of its problems. It's got both access codes. That's the incredible thing.

They wait for a moment in silence. Squeaking. Then:

Aladdin Michael John Shepherd. Sex male. Date of birth thirteen eleven thirty-six. Consultant Mr Jonathan Grey. Complaint tachycardia paroxysma.

Steven What the hell's that?

Julia Involuntary speeding of the heart.

Aladdin Treatment point one five grams tabs digoxyn.

Steven Is that correct?

Julia Yes. He has to take three a day.

Steven And digoxyn is a . . .

Julia Digitalis derivative.

Aladdin Do you wish to kill Michael John Shepherd?

Julia (*keying in*) Yes.

Aladdin Move decimal point one point to right.

Julia (*to Steven*) How do I do that?

Steven Well, you move the cursor up to the treatment line, then along.

Julia The what?

Steven This little correction symbol. It's called the cursor. (*He moves the little correction blob along until it reaches the figures*)

Julia Isn't that extraordinary. I can kill my husband with a cursor.

Aladdin Awaiting instructions. Escape or enter?

Julia (*keying in*) Enter.

Aladdin Verify update. Point one five times ten equals one point five grams tabs digoxyn. Massive overdose. Death by cardiac failure. Disconnecting. Line now clear.

"Pop Goes the Weasel " on synthesizer

Steven So . . . the next time he calls at the hospital for his heart pills he gets issued ten times the dose.

Julia He'd never query it. He has a blind faith in his specialist. As a matter of fact, he has an appointment to see him tomorrow.

Steven Ah, suppose he goes to his doctor instead?

Julia He doesn't. He sees his specialist routinely the first Tuesday of every month for a check-up. It's usually just a formality, then he goes down to the dispensary to collect his medication.

Steven So . . . the hospital commits the murder for you.

Julia Suppose the dispensary gets suspicious and checks the dose back?

Steven So what? The computer confirms it as accurate.

Julia But such a high dose . . .

Steven What's a high dose for one patient could be quite normal for another. Anyway, hospitals these days are dishing out pills all day long. They don't know the face at the window.

Julia But there'd be an enquiry afterwards, and if they find out the clinical records have been changed . . .

Steven That's easy to cover up. As soon as you know the victim has taken his pills, you get Aladdin to move that decimal point back to its original position. And there's no trace it was ever tampered with.

Julia Then it really would be the perfect murder.

Steven Just about as perfect as any murder can be. You might even try suing the hospital for negligence.

Julia I don't think I'd risk that somehow.

Steven (*admiringly to Aladdin*) Nice one Aladdin. That's a very smart little game you've got there . . . Well, I suppose I'd better move that decimal point back again hadn't I? (*He laughs*) Before you end up as the first computer widow.

Julia Yes . . . I suppose you should.

Steven seats himself at the computer in no great hurry, then looks across at Julia quizzically, his fingers poised. It is a little temptation game. She takes a deep breath

On the other hand Michael doesn't go for his appointment until ten o'clock tomorrow so there's no great rush . . .

Steven (*cautiously*) No?

Julia It would be fun to contemplate the thought of being a widow . . . for just one night . . .

Steven You mean to contemplate revenge?

Julia It's only a game after all.

Steven But of course. (*Casually*) Pity we're not playing for money.

Julia We could be.

Steven Oh yes . . . like . . . how much?

Julia A quarter of a million?

Steven (*quietly*) You are joking of course, my lovely?

Julia No.

Steven (*trying to sound as casual as her*) Well now, that could come in handy.

Julia What for?

Steven Oh . . . just to snatch a fleeting thought out of the air . . . to launch Steven Jones Software International.

She raises an eyebrow. He adds hastily

Which naturally would then become Shepherd Jones International. Equal partnership . . . both active and sleeping.

Julia Then all our dreams would come true wouldn't they, Mr Jones?

He crosses to her and puts an arm round her neck snuggling her cheek

Steven Too bloody right, Mrs Shepherd.

She gets up and they walk slowly to the interior exit

But as you said ... it's only a game.

The Lights start to fade

Julia Only a game ...

The Lights fade to Black-out

CURTAIN

ACT II

The same. Morning

A certain amount of tidying up has taken place. The Greenpeace whale poster has gone. The computer remains in the same position

Julia is in the kitchen area

Steven enters. He carries a bunch of flowers

Steven Morning lovely.
Julia Where have you been?
Steven A long walk round the back lanes.
Julia You said you'd be back by half-past nine.
Steven Ah, I'm sorry. These are for you. Is there any breakfast?
Julia And what have you done to this room?
Steven Just tidied up a bit, that's all.
Julia Who asked you to?
Steven If this is going to be the general office of Jones and Shepherd Software Great Britain Incorporated plc it's got to be suitable for receiving clients. Anyway I thought you'd be pleased.
Julia Where's my "Save the Whale" poster?
Steven Oh I moved it. It ruined the decor.
Julia (*firmly*) Where is it?
Steven Basically, in the loo.
Julia In the loo?
Steven I thought it might appreciate the sound of running water.
Julia It's a deep sea mammal, not a bloody salmon.
Steven So, it's all right to kill husbands, but not whales.
Julia Whales are an endangered species.
Steven So are husbands by the sound of it.
Julia Only my own, I've no intention of wiping out the entire husband species.
Steven Why not? With that handy little murder program, you could be the heroine of the feminist ecology movement.
Julia God! I've ended up with another sexist pig.
Steven I'm only joking. Just relax, my lovely . . .
Julia How can I bloody relax! He'll be on his way to the hospital by now . . .
Steven Now take your mind off it. All you have to do is keep calm. Everything's going to be fine. Look, he's on great form.

Aladdin plays the tune "Pop Goes the Weasel"

Julia For God's sake! You're like a little kid with that thing.

Steven Don't disconnect Aladdin, sweetheart. We still need him. It's not over yet.

Julia I wish it was. I can't stand this waiting.

Steven (*putting his arm round her*) I know, I know. But it's going to be worth it in the end. Just relax and sit down. Now, tell me about your husband. All those awful things.

Julia Why?

Steven For heaven's sake, Julia. If I'm to help kill the poor sod I'm entitled to know something about him.

Julia I completely fail to see the logic of that. I would have thought it's a great deal easier to kill someone you don't know the first thing about.

Steven I wouldn't know. I've never done this before. (*Picking up photographs*) Is this him?

Julia Yes, where did you find those?

Steven (*absorbed*) Now that's interesting. You threw out his clothes, but not his photographs.

Julia What deep meaning do you read into that?

Steven That you're still in love with him?

Julia I just haven't got around to chucking them out yet, that's all.

Steven Hmmmmm . . . very ordinary-looking man, isn't he?

Julia What did you expect?

Steven I don't know. The way you've been talking about him, a sort of cross between Rudolf Valentino and Stalin. Is this the wedding?

Julia (*drily*) No, we used to dress up like that every day.

Steven Who's the pretty little bridesmaid?

Julia Alex.

Steven You left it a bit late, didn't you? She must be at least ten.

Julia She's from his first marriage.

Steven Oh? What broke that up?

Julia Infidelity.

Steven On whose part?

Julia His.

Steven Anyone you knew?

Julia Me.

Steven Oh. You should have been warned then, shouldn't you?

Julia crosses to him, snatches the photographs out of his hand and throws them in the fireplace

Julia Stop grubbing around in my past.

Steven I'm fascinated. So it was his second marriage and your . . . what . . . first?

Julia And last.

Steven So, Alex is your stepdaughter.

Julia Obviously.

Steven And you never had any children of your own . . .

Julia just ignores the remark

Why was that, choice or bad luck?

mind your own bus...

Julia (*snapping at him*) What makes men think all women want to have children?

Steven In other words, bad luck.

Julia Mind your own business.

Steven Well, if I'm to be your lover, Julia, I'm entitled to know a bit more about you.

Julia Some other time. (*She glances at her watch*) It's five to ten. He'll be arriving at reception about now. He's a stickler for time . . . he may even have gone up to the clinic to try to get first in the queue.

Steven (*shrugging*) Well, I suppose the sooner he gets there the sooner it's over.

She suddenly gets up, her manner quite changed now, all apprehension gone

Julia Steven, it is time to put our little murder game back in its box.

Steven What do you mean?

Julia I can't go through with it. It's as simple as that.

Steven You really are a very changeable woman, Mrs Shepherd. You've kept me up half the night relishing the sweet revenge you are going to take on your husband, how he's lied to you all your life and how he deserves to die. And now, when it's just within our grasp, you want out.

Julia Don't you?

Steven Me? Certainly not, I'll try anything once.

Julia Steven Jones, if my husband were to walk through that door now and you had a loaded gun, would you shoot him? Here, in front of my eyes?

Steven Well, you could always turn your back.

Julia Could you, or could you not kill a man in cold blood?

Steven (*starting to flounder a little*) Well . . . this is a different situation, isn't it . . .

Julia How is it different? Because you can just press a key on that electronic assassin and never see the victim? How is that different, Steven?

Steven (*starting to back down*) Well obviously, I wouldn't want to go through with it if you didn't want me to . . . I mean he's your husband after all . . .

Julia (*checking her watch again*) It's two minutes to ten.

Steven So what do you want me to do?

Julia Instruct that infernal machine to call it off. To undo the murder plan PLEASE!!

Steven (*suddenly leaping into action, as though himself now greatly relieved*) I wish you'd told me before! (*He starts to key instructions*)

Aladdin responds with a whirring, squeaking sound as it goes through its code strings

Julia What's it doing now?

Steven Going back to the beginning. We have to re-programme.

The squeaking stops. Aladdin plays the tune "Good-morning, good-morning"

Damn! It's gone right back to the main menu . . .

Aladdin Hallo Penny. How are you today?

Julia Get on with it!
Aladdin Hallo Pamela.
Steven Damn!
Aladdin Hallo Juliet.
Julia What's the problem?
Aladdin Hallo Margaret.
Steven I can't remember the file it's in.
Aladdin Hallo Cynthia.
Julia MURDER.
Aladdin Hallo Janice.
Steven That's the program title. I need the file first.
Aladdin Hallo Jemima.
Julia GAMES. TRY GAMES!
Aladdin Hallo Doreen. Hallo Rosalind.
Steven (*keying in*) Ah, that's it. ~~Thanks very much.~~ GAMES.
Aladdin Would you like to play a game, Julia?
Steven (*keying "yes"*) Of course she bloody does!
Aladdin Which game?
Steven (*keying*) Murder. Come on!
Julia ⎫ (*together*) There must be a way of by-passing all this.
Aladdin ⎭ Who do you wish to murder, Julia?

Steven ⎫ (*together*) That's what I'm trying to do, if you'd just hang on a
Aladdin ⎭ minute.
Age. Sex. Motive.
Julia ⎫ (*together*) We haven't got a minute. It's ten o'clock.
Aladdin ⎭ Select from: One: money. Two: jealousy—

Furious squeaking from Aladdin, followed by the "Dead March in Saul"

Steven Shit! It's gone back to the beginning. Pass me the manual, quick.
Julia Where is it?
Steven In my bloody briefcase!!
Aladdin The murder game. The murder game. The murder game . . . *etc.*
Julia (*shouting*) God in heaven! You call yourself a computer expert!
Steven (*shouting back*) If you'd stop breathing down my neck, woman, I'd
have a chance to think!
Julia Get on with it.
Steven (*looking through the manual*) It's a GO TO instruction. Of course. A
simple bloody GO TO! (*He keys*) GO TO C R A C CODE.

The tune ends

Aladdin C R A C CODE two seven seven eight Cromwell SX-one. Attach
modem. Attach modem. Attach modem . . . *etc.*
Julia What?
Steven Attach the sodding telephone.

*Julia crosses quickly to the telephone but the moment before she reaches it, it
starts to ring. She stands there, hand out for the receiver but not touching it,
frozen*

Don't stand there like a paralysed rabbit! Clear the line.

She picks it up, holds it to her ear for a second, unable to speak. Steven gets up and crosses to her, snatching the receiver from her hand

(*Into the phone*) You have a wrong number. Clear the line.

He slams down the receiver for a couple of seconds, then lifts it up again. The line clear sound is heard. Steven puts it on the modem cradle, then returns to the keyboard

Aladdin Wait please.

A dialling sound is heard. They both stay frozen, watching it. After a few seconds, the engaged signal is heard

All lines engaged.

Julia puts her head in her hands

Julia No ... I don't believe this! (*Then she shouts at Steven*) Tell it to keep trying!
Steven It does it automatically ...
Aladdin Wait please.

Dialling is heard again

Julia It's doing it on purpose, isn't it. Deliberately prevaricating.
Aladdin All lines engaged.
Steven Don't talk rot, woman ...

Dialling

Julia How the hell do you know what it's up to? I wouldn't trust that evil machine further than I could spit!
Aladdin All lines engaged.
Julia It's lying, I tell you, it's lying! It's trying to kill my husband whether I want it or not!

Dialling

Steven Bullshit ...

She crosses to the modem to pick up the receiver. Steven gets up to stop her

Aladdin All lines engaged.
Steven What the hell do you think you're doing?
Julia I'm going to call the hospital myself!
Steven (*grabbing her wrist*) No, wait!
Aladdin Line now clear. Reconnecting C R A C CODE two seven seven eight CROMWELL SX-one.

Steven immediately rushes back to the keyboard

Steven (*keying in*) Display.

Now it is Steven's turn to start to lose his nerve

Display, you bastard!

A sudden, continuous high-pitched buzzing sound, then:

Aladdin DEADLY EMBRACE. DEADLY EMBRACE. DEADLY EM-
BRACE.
Steven Oh, Christ!
Julia What does that mean? (*She screams at him*) I asked what it means?!
Steven It means that someone else is trying to scan the same clinical records
at precisely the same time. The two computers are locking each other out.
Julia What?
Steven Deadly embrace is like two people trying to get through a doorway
at the same time. Neither can move till one gives way . . .
Aladdin Access obtainable . . .
Steven It's all right . . . it's clear now. Someone has stepped back.
Aladdin Michael John Shepherd. Sex male. Date of birth thirteen eleven
thirty-nine. Consultant Mr Jonathan Grey. Complaint tachycardia par-
oxysma. Treatment point one five tabs digoxyn.

There is a beat before Julia cries out

Julia It's back. Back to the original!
Steven Well . . . that's what you wanted . . .
Julia (*a beat*) But who did it?
Steven It must have been Grey, or some suspicious character in the
dispensary.
Julia They might start an enquiry?
Steven I told you it can't be checked back. There's no trail. (*He shrugs*)
They're more likely to put it down to typing error or a bug in the system.
Julia Oh, Steven. I never want to go through a nightmare like that again.
Let's get out of this house. I feel stifled. (*She takes his hand and tries to pull
him away*)
Steven I'm not leaving this house with that program still in the memory.
Julia Doesn't matter now, does it? It's only a game . . .
Steven I'm not taking any chances. (*He keys in*) Delete murder menu.
Aladdin Are you sure?
Julia What did it ask for?
Steven Standard practice. Just in case you weren't sure.
Julia (*to Aladdin*) Do as you're told, you bloodthirsty little beast.
Steven (*keying in*) Yes.

Squeaking and whirring from Aladdin. Then silence

Right, lovely. It's all gone now. Disappeared without trace. There never
was a murder game.
Julia Oh, Steven, thank God!
Steven And I'm still as poor as a church mouse.
Julia Never mind, I like church mice. Paris! Let's go to Paris for a couple of
days.
Steven Oh, yes, what with?

Julia I'll treat you. (*Crossing to exit*) We'll get a few things in a bag and just go!

Steven Oh, well in that case. I've never been to Paris . . . I'll take a shower first. (*To Aladdin*) Right, now you behave yourself while we're away. Huh?

The Lights fade to Black-out. Computer chatter

SCENE 2

The same. Two days later

The room is the same as in the previous scene except that there are letters on the mat and two copies of the "Cambridge News". The computer is dark and silent

Julia enters in smart travelling clothes, carrying a small suitcase and stoops to pick up the papers and mail from the door mat

The telephone rings. She crosses to it but does not answer. As Julia stoops to the phone it stops ringing. We hear a taxi door slam and the engine as it drives away. Julia rifles through the mail, but they are mainly brown envelopes and presumably bills, so she sets them aside and starts looking through the newspapers

Steven enters. He carries a larger suitcase, older and rather more battered

Steven Was that the phone?

Julia Yes, stopped before I reached it.

Steven That usually happens to me. And I just know it's the vital call that might have changed my life . . . Well, I may not be any richer, but at least I'm getting my oats regular.

Julia Pig. (*She puts down the first paper and starts to scan through the second*)

Steven What are you looking for?

Julia Just catching up with the local news.

Steven Come on . . . you've been edgy since we left Paris. What do you expect to find?

Julia Michael was the key speaker at an economics seminar yesterday at the Granta Court Hotel . . . I just wondered if he was there, that's all.

Steven And was he?

Julia Apparently not . . . at least, he isn't mentioned.

Steven Perhaps he's in Honolulu by now with his lady friend.

Julia It's not like him to miss an opportunity to pontificate before his peers.

Steven So what are you trying to say?

Julia Nothing really . . .

Steven Then stop worrying about it, eh?

Julia I'm not. I really couldn't care less. (*She throws away the paper*) Coffee?

Steven Lovely . . . Nice being waited on . . .

Julia Don't bank on it in the future. I wonder why Liz didn't go to Paris?

Steven picks up one of the evening papers and starts to scan through it himself.
Julia is filling the percolator with water and coffee. There is a pause, then:

Steven I mean if anything had happened to him, someone would have to
   know where to contact your daughter, I assume.
Julia Yes, of course.
Steven But on the other hand, she didn't know you were in Paris.
Julia She'd have been waiting here for me or left a note.
Steven Oh yes. Naturally. (*A beat*) When is she due home, by the way?
Julia Why?
Steven Oh, I don't know. I just wondered how you're going to explain me?
Julia How would you like to be explained?
Steven I don't know. You could say you'd taken in a lodger, I suppose ...
   to help out financially.
Julia Roger the lodger?
Steven Or a student, that's it. I could be a computer technology student.
   That would also explain Aladdin.
Julia I shall simply say that you're my stud.
Steven What, to your daughter?
Julia Why not?
Steven Well ... she might think I'm a bit young for you ... I mean ...
Julia Yes. Carry on.
Steven (*hastily*) Not that that makes any difference, I mean if two people
   love one another ... like.
Julia And do they?
Steven Well, we certainly fancy one another ... I mean ... don't we?
Julia Go on.
Steven (*floundering around in water far too deep for him*) At what point
   precisely sex turns into love ... or the other way round, I wouldn't know.
   I mean, I don't have that much experience.
Julia Oh, such modesty Steven Jones.
Steven (*quickly*) Well, I must admit I did feel the first stirrings ... as we were
   crossing the Pont Neuf last night ... hand in hand ...
Julia Now, that's more like my beloved bullshit artist.
Steven (*taking her in his arms*) No honestly, I really mean it.
Julia And it's not because I remind you of your mother.
Steven Oh definitely not! She's a lot fatter than you.
Julia Sweet boy.
Steven And what about you? Any similar stirrings up your end of the tent?
   Or am I just a pick-up—still on seven day trial.
Julia I need you Steven. We'll just have to see what follows from that.

The phone rings. They break apart

   Would you answer that?
Steven It's bound to be for you.
Julia The coffee's ready. (*She crosses to the now percolating coffee pot, glad
   of the excuse not to go near the phone*)
Steven I'll do the coffee.

Julia (*sharply*) Answer it.

He shrugs and crosses to the phone

Steven (*into the phone*) Hallo ... Er—Mrs Shepherd ... Yes, she is here. Who's calling?
Julia Who is it?
Steven (*cupping the phone; to Julia*) The Granta Court Hotel ...
Julia What do they want?
Steven (*shrugging*) Ask them.

He holds out the receiver to her. She takes it, cautiously, tentatively

Julia (*into the phone*) Hallo ... Yes—I'm sorry there's been no answer, but I've been away for a few days. ... Yes. ... (*Her voice goes flat*) What have you found? ... I see—look, do you think you could bring it round in a taxi? I'll pay of course. ... Thank you. Goodbye.

She puts the receiver down slowly, her body tense, her face drawn. For a moment she says nothing. Steven looks at her

Steven Bring what round in a taxi?
Julia Michael's hand luggage.
Steven (*in relief*) For a moment I thought you meant the corpse.
Julia He checked out two days ago. He told the desk he had a hospital appointment that morning but he'd be back to collect his things ... He never returned.
Steven (*after a pause*) Well. That's it, then. We were too late after all.
Julia But someone changed that dose back again ...
Steven Then they must have been too late as well ...
Julia But if he is dead, where is he ... I mean ... the body?
Steven Some morgue somewhere ... or a hospital ... he could be in the Gobi desert. What does it matter? Someone will be in touch soon.
Julia My God ... so it's done.
Steven That's right. It's done. And there's no turning back now. (*The coffee making now forgotten, he crosses over to comfort her*) Now come on. You tried to stop it, we both did. Fate conspired. So cheer up, lovely. You're a rich widow after all. How does it feel.
Julia Awful.
Steven Well, never mind. You'll get over it. Think of the great times we'll have together. Not just a couple of days in Paris. A whole month on the Riviera. We'll go to the Caribbean and drink planters punch till it comes out of our ears. Take a felucca up the Nile to see the Valley of Kings ... Build a jacuzzi in the back garden and bathe naked amongst the pulsing jets. How does that grab you?
Julia (*forcing a smile*) Sounds like London Airport.
Steven (*with immense cheerfulness*) Right. That's settled then. I think I'll go and have a shower. (*He starts to move to exit*)
~~**Julia** Pontius Pilate.~~
~~**Steven** What?~~
~~**Julia** I never knew a man who needed so many showers.~~

Steven (*lapsing into broad valleys Welsh*) Making up for lost time, see. When I was a boy in Glygofachmayant we never had showers. They'd nicked all our water for Liverpool. No flush toilets either. So we had to piss in the reservoir.

Julia I do love you, Steven Jones.

Steven exits to the bathroom

Julia crosses slowly to the mirror to look at her face. She pushes back her long hair and gazes blankly into her own eyes as though exorcizing a bad dream

Liz (*off*) Hallo! (*She knocks*) Hallo Julia darling, I'm back!

Liz enters the front door. She is dressed in the latest Paris fashions and looks a million dollars

Where are you?

Julia comes down to the bottom step

Oh, there you are! How are you bearing up? (*She takes a good look at Julia*) My God you look positively shagged out.

Julia Do I?

Liz What have you been up to? Moping around the house feeling sorry for yourself, I suppose.

Julia Something like that. How was Paris?

Liz Oh, I survived. Boring fashion show, but I bought some schmutters.

Julia (*looking at her costume*) Fabulous. That must have set you back a few francs.

Liz Trade, darling. How do you like my tan?

Julia Amazing. Bottle or pills?

Liz Sheer hard work, darling. I slipped on down to Cannes for a twenty-four hour roasting. Would you believe, starkers?

Julia Really?

Liz One has to these days, darling. The beach is full of bloody Rhine-maidens with tits like grapefruits and bums like plums. We British have to show the flag. (*She looks round the room, suddenly realizes it has changed*) My godfathers! What's happened to this room? It's tidy!

Julia So?

Liz Darling, do you feel all right?

Steven enters from the bathroom, dripping wet, with a towel wrapped round his loins

Steven (*to Julia*) Have you got a shirt I can borrow, lovely? (*Then seeing Liz*) Oh, I'm sorry . . .

Liz Oh not at all. (*She looks him up and down*) Well, hallo . . . whoever you are.

Julia Oh . . . Steven, this is my friend Liz. Liz . . . Steven . . .

Liz (*to Julia*) Well, that explains everything. (*To Steven*) Are you the plumber?

Steven No I was just having a shower.

Liz The twenty-four hour kind she mentioned on the phone.

Steven No . . . I'm a high-technology specialist.

Liz How useful. Do you put up bookshelves?

Julia (*quickly*) His speciality is re-arranging them.

Liz (*to Steven*) Oh, so *you're* responsible for this amazing transformation. How did you get away with it? I've been trying to tidy her up for years. Julia is the all-time, original slut, aren't you darling?

Julia Steven, go and get dressed.

Liz Why? He looks fine to me as he is. Like that statue by Michaelangelo. The one with the big stone—

Julia (*cutting in*) Get dressed, Steven!

Steven Yes. (*He goes to exit again*)

Julia (*calling after him*) There's a shirt in the airing cupboard.

Steven Ah . . .

Steven exits

Liz (*looking at Julia with genuine admiration*) Well you certainly didn't waste much time. Isn't he gorgeous? And so obedient. Did he arrive fully trained or have you had him on a choke lead?

Julia (*firmly*) He's not for you, Liz.

Liz Not even for the odd weekend?

Julia Not even for the odd weekend.

Liz That's mean. Don't forget it was me who suggested you take a lover.

Julia I know. And I'm very grateful. But not *that* grateful.

Liz Where did you find him?

Julia He came to sell me some computer equipment.

Liz Of course . . . you mentioned your computer on the phone. (*Looking at the screen*) What does it do—show blue movies?

Julia It's called the Aladdin Genie, and it gives three wishes.

Liz How many have you used up so far?

Julia One.

Liz Well, if you've got a wish you're not using, darling, I'd like to be tall, twenty-three with tits like grapefruits and a bum like a little ripe plum. (*To the computer*) Could you manage that for me, Aladdin?

Julia I don't think it's that clever.

Liz Oh, thanks a bunch! Seriously, darling. What are you supposed to do with it?

Julia Steven and I are thinking of going into the computer software business.

Liz But that's terrific! You really are getting it together . . . handsome lover, new career, tidy. It must feel like being born again.

Julia Yes, it does, a little.

Liz Have you heard from your ex at all?

Julia Michael? No. Why should I?

Liz Just thought he might have had a change of heart. That's all.

Julia It's rather late for that now.

Knocking at the front door

Excuse me. (*She goes to answer the door*) Would you like to help yourself
to a drink.
Liz Thank you darling. I thought you'd never ask.

Liz helps herself to vodka/tonic/ice while Julia answers the door

Receptionist Mrs Shepherd?
Julia Yes.
Receptionist Your husband's things.
Julia Thank you. (*Giving the girl £10 from her handbag*) Keep the change.
Receptionist Thank you, madam. And I presume this is yours. (*She hands
over an envelope*) Goodbye.

The Receptionist exits

Julia shuts the door and comes slowly back, opening the envelope

Liz Have you been away, darling?
Julia Just for a break.
Liz Anywhere nice?
Julia Paris.
Liz Then why on earth didn't you look me up?
Julia We tried, but couldn't find you. Where were you staying?
Liz Er ... er ...

Steven enters from the interior, now fully dressed in slacks and shirt

Steven Ah ...
Julia Steven, would you be an angel and go and get a bottle of vodka?
Steven We got two in duty free and there's one in the fridge ... and it's
pissing down with rain!
Julia (*sharply*) Steven. Liz and I want a confidential chat.
Steven Oh, well why didn't you say so before ...

Steven exits

Liz Actually darling, I can't stop. I just wanted to make sure you were all
right.
Julia (*ignoring the remark*) I thought you would be staying at Le Gorgon,
you always stay there, don't you? So Steven and I booked in there too.
Liz Oh, I'd probably gone down to Cannes by that time. What a shame.
Julia I asked at the desk. They said you'd cancelled and weren't coming to
France at all.
Liz Oh, they never know what's going on at that hotel. Listen, I really must
go ...

Julia settles Liz down again

Julia You asked me if I'd heard from Michael. I haven't, at least not
directly. But I know where he's been for the last few days.
Liz Do you?
Julia The Granta Court Hotel. (*After a fraction's pause*) In a double room.
Booked in the name of Mr and Mrs Shepherd.

Liz Oh that's a bit much.

Julia Isn't it. He appears to have left in a bit of a hurry . . . leaving a few personal belongings behind. Which includes . . . (*She takes an ear-ring out of the envelope*) One of your ear-rings. It must have slipped beneath the pillow.

Liz (*taking it gingerly*) Oh . . . (*Then with a nervous laugh*) Not one of mine, darling. Very similar, but—

Julia Which I gave you for your last birthday.

Liz (*after a fraction's pause, then resigned*) So? You'd finished with him.

Julia How long has this been going on?

Liz You'd thrown him out. He was anybody's . . .

Julia Six months? A year . . . ?

Liz Two and a half years.

Julia What!

Liz You asked.

Julia My best friend.

Liz Your marriage has been over for ages, darling. You just couldn't admit it to yourself. I'm sorry . . .

Julia Cuddles! Of course, I should have realized! It was you, you bitch. My God! You've sat in my kitchen year after year. Drunk my vodka, told me all the sordid details of your boring sex life except for one thing. That you were screwing my husband.

Liz Only occasionally. When he was away at a conference.

Julia Occasionally! Occasionally makes it all right, I suppose.

Liz And not at all in the past six months.

Julia What were you doing on Monday night? Watching the bloody television?!

Liz Now just calm down, Julia. You're getting yourself into a state again.

Julia If anyone else tells me to calm down I'm going to throttle them.

Liz You're going to find this very hard to take Julia, but if you want to know the truth, it's me that's been keeping your marriage together these past few years.

Julia (*incredulous*) Say that again!

Liz Now please listen to me. He was going to leave you two years ago. It was me who persuaded him not to. And half a dozen times since then . . .

Julia (*almost in tears now*) You expect me to believe that?

Liz Yes. Because it's true. I told him he was behaving like an irresponsible pig. That it was cruel to you and potentially harmful to Alex . . .

Julia Oh, thank you very much!!!

Liz Just face up to the facts for once in your life. If I'd wanted to take him away from you I could have done it at any time. I'm sorry . . . but that's not what I wanted for him, or for you, or for me. I just wanted everything to stay as it was. He'd stay married to you and the family would stay together.

Julia And you'd go on screwing him behind my back!

Liz It was all very discreet. Besides, he was on the loose. If I hadn't grabbed him somebody else would have done.

Julia It's the deceit. Don't you understand, I can't bear being deceived.

Liz Then I'm sorry to say this darling, but it's time you grew up. You've got bookshelves full of European literature and you haven't learnt a thing from it. If men didn't deceive women, and women didn't deceive women, most of those great classics would never have been written. There'd have been no novelists and Shakespeare would have stayed a second-rate actor, like Ronald Reagan.

Julia I don't live my life out of romantic fiction.

Liz You'd be a lot less neurotic if you did. Look what's happening to the Americans. You've only got to brush up against someone at a New York party and he belts straight back to his wife and tells her he's been unfaithful and wants a divorce. And before you can turn around there's half a dozen homeless kids and a bill from the lawyers that cripples you for life. People don't know how to handle marriage any more.

Julia Oh God, look who's talking!

Liz I learnt. Too late. Listen, do you want to know why I went to see Michael that night?

Julia No.

Liz Then I'll tell you. I went to persuade him to come back to you. All right, so we ended up in bed because that's the way things happen. I spent half the night trying to make him see sense. I told him "Michael, it's Julia you really love. I'm just your bit on the side. Get yourself sorted out. Go home and say you're sorry and ask her to take you back." And you know something? He agreed.

Julia What?

Liz He agreed. He's coming back to you, darling. You can both have a lovely tearful reconciliation.

Julia I don't believe a word of this.

Liz Then ask him. I don't understand why he's not already here.

Julia (*suddenly blurting out*) Because he's dead.

Steven appears in the entrance, a bottle of vodka in his hand

Liz What?

Julia (*now totally losing control*) He's dead! I killed him. (*Then seeing Steven frozen in the doorway*) No . . . that isn't strictly true. *We* killed him. Didn't we, Steven? Go on tell her. Tell her how we killed her precious lover!

Steven Julia, you don't know what you're saying!

Julia Go on, tell the smug bitch!!!

Steven slaps Julia

Steven She doesn't know what she's saying. She's delirious. Now, now now. Who have we been killing today? Now come on and sit down and take one of your pills . . .

Julia I haven't got any more pills . . .

Steven Right. Well, then I'll get you a glass of brandy . . . (*He crosses to the kitchen. To Liz*) Would you make the bed? She needs a good rest.

Liz All right. (*Liz goes upstairs*) I think she's heading for a breakdown. She's been on the edge of it for months.

Liz switches on the bedroom lights

Julia Steven ...
Steven Coming, darling ...

Liz pulls up the duvet and as she does so, Michael's dead body, so far concealed beneath, reveals itself, slipping half-way over the edge of the bed

Julia Michael ... Michael ...

Black-out

Scene 3

The same. The following day

Odd squeaking noises from the computer form into a polyphonic tune, "Abide With Me"

The Lights come up to show Steven in the kitchen filling the kettle at the sink. He then crosses to the computer

Aladdin Funeral arrangements check list. Have you ... One: informed the victim's personal doctor.
Steven (*keying in*) Yes.
Aladdin Two: obtained death certificate.
Steven Yes.
Aladdin Three: had body removed to morgue.
Steven Bloody quick.
Aladdin Four: contacted funeral director.
Steven Yes.
Aladdin Five: informed executors.
Steven Not known.
Aladdin Six: reported death to registrar.
Steven In process.
Aladdin Seven: informed relatives.
Steven Yes. Daughter.
Aladdin Eight: read the will.
Steven No not yet.
Julia (*calling, off, from the interior*) Steven!
Steven (*calling back*) Yes I'm here.
Aladdin Nine: ordered flowers.

Julia enters in her night-dress and dressing-gown, still half-asleep

Steven Oh, shut up! (*He turns Aladdin off*)
Julia (*rubbing sleep from her eyes*) How long have I been asleep?
Steven (*glancing at his watch*) Nearly twenty-four hours. Liz gave you a couple of sleeping pills, and we put you in the spare room. We didn't think you'd want to go up there again.
Julia (*still confused*) What's been happening?
Steven (*indicating the VDU screen*) It's all there.

Julia glances at the screen

Julia Who put that on? You?

Steven I just provided the answers. Aladdin supplied the check list.

Julia Yes but where did it come from?

Steven It's part of the murder program.

Julia I thought you said you'd wiped that program out.

Steven I wiped out the first part. The actual murder, but now it seems there's a second part. Funeral arrangements. It's an amazingly comprehensive program.

Julia Then why the hell haven't you wiped that out as well?

Steven I'm using it. It's all right, it's quite harmless. As a matter of fact, I thought I might put it on a floppy and market it. Everyone needs a handypack funeral menu for when their relatives pop off. I could make a fortune.

Julia I don't want anything left on that damn machine. It could give us away.

Steven (*laughing*) You talk about giving us away. Who started blabbing to Liz about us killing your husband?

Julia Did I? God!

Steven Luckily, she thought you'd gone off your head. Which I was happy to confirm.

Julia How's Liz now?

Steven She's rushing around making herself useful. She's in her element.

Julia I bet she is.

Steven She's also rung your daughter. She should be here tomorrow.

Julia What about ... the body?

Steven It's in the linen cupboard.

Julia What?

Steven With Colonel Mustard. My little joke! Look, everything is being dealt with.

Julia (*looking at the list*) What does it say on the death certificate?

Steven A load of old Greek really, but it all boils down to heart failure.

Julia Heart failure ... did the doctor see his pills?

Steven No. I managed to make them lose themselves.

Julia You mean he doesn't know how it happened?

Steven Well if he thinks it's a perfectly normal heart attack, who are we to argue?

Julia They'll find out at the post-mortem.

Steven He says there's no need for one. He knows your husband had a history of heart trouble. He reckons he probably ran upstairs too fast and blew his ticker. He reports to the coroner and we can go ahead with the burial.

Julia You mean ... we've been driving ourselves mad with worry for nothing?

Steven No *you* have. Not me. I always told you it would work out all right.

Julia Oh Steven, I can't believe this! So we didn't kill him after all.

Steven What?

Julia You just told me. Heart failure. A perfectly normal death ... it's unbelievable!

Steven No, my lovely. It is believable, apparently. But it doesn't happen to be true.

Julia Nonsense. I accept the doctor's version. I'm sure that's how it happened. I always told Michael not to run upstairs . . .

Steven You really are amazing. You believe just anything you want to believe, if it happens to be convenient.

Julia We are free, Steven. Free of responsibility, free of guilt. Our life together begins today, and it's going to be amazing.

Steven Yes, well . . . we really have to finish this check list first. Any idea who the executors are? I mean the executors . . .

Julia (*going to look in the chest upstage*) They'll be named in the will. It should be among his private papers.

Steven Liz couldn't find it.

Julia Liz! You surely didn't let Liz go through all my private documents.

Steven She was only trying to help.

Julia I bet she was, the nosy bitch.

Liz enters the front door. She carries a supermarket carrier bag

Liz Julia, darling. You shouldn't be up. You're not well.

Julia I'm perfectly well, thank you.

Liz (*to Steven*) Hallo love. (*To Julia*) You always did have amazing powers of recovery. But you mustn't overdo it. You're still in shock.

Julia I'm feeling quite recovered now, thank you.

Liz (*to Steven*) How are you doing, lover boy?

Steven Not bad. Just got to take the death certificate to the registrar, order the flowers, then we're ready.

Liz You'd better go and do the flowers now.

Steven Oh, everybody's bloody errand boy round here, aren't I?

Liz Go Steven.

Steven (*going to the front door*) What kind of flowers would you like, lovely?

Julia (*impatiently*) Just leave it to the florist.

Steven (*as he exits*) I'll see if they have any forget-me-nots.

Steven exits

Liz What are you looking for, darling. The will?

Julia How did you guess?

Liz (*fishing in her handbag*) Not to worry. I've got it. It was lodged with his solicitors.

Julia How did you get hold of it? They had no right to pass it over.

Liz It seems Michael named me as an executor, darling. (*She hands Julia the will*)

Julia Why aren't I an executor? (*She starts to scan down the will*)

Liz Oh, I never think it's a good idea to name the wife as an executor. She has so much on her mind at the time of bereavement. Besides, it's a boring job and you need a head for business. Obviously Michael thought that as well.

But Julia is too busy scanning down the will to respond, so Liz adds reassuringly

But you've got nothing to worry about. He's left you everything. House, car, telly, stereo—even the gardening tools. So he wasn't really such a bad old bugger after all. (*She pauses*) And then of course, there's the insurance money.

Julia (*glancing up*) What did you say?

Liz The insurance money, darling. Don't tell me you'd forgotten that.

Julia Oh ... no ... that'll be quite useful.

Liz I'm sure it will. (*She holds out her hand for the will again*) Now you've read it, could I have it back?

Julia Why?

Liz Darling, that's what executors are for. They have to take charge of everything. The will, the bills, the funeral arrangements. Even the body.

Julia The body!

Liz Didn't you know that?

Julia But he's my husband.

Liz Was.

Julia He's mine.

Liz Not any more. Once a man's dead, the body no longer belongs to the widow. It's placed in the hands of his executors, who arrange for its disposal. (*She takes the will from Julia*) So you can safely leave all that to me.

Julia (*quickly*) I'm sure he'd have wanted to be cremated.

Liz Oh no, Michael told me that when he died he was going to leave his body to medicine.

Julia To what?

Liz To the medical profession, darling ... spare parts. In case someone happens to be looking for an odd kidney or a second-hand toe. It's terribly trendy.

Julia I won't have it. I absolutely refuse to allow it. It's ghoulish.

Alex enters

Alex What's ghoulish, Mother?

Liz Oh, Alex, you're here. You OK? Listen, darling could you persuade your mother to be reasonable? Your poor dear father wants to donate his mortal remains to the hospital and she wants him turned to ashes, or something equally biodegradable. What do you think?

Alex I think we have to carry out Daddy's wishes. (*To Julia*) And I don't see why you should object to that, Mother, after all, it's a form of immortality—and socially useful.

Liz (*to Julia*) There, darling, I'm sure you'd have wanted your husband to be socially useful at the last knockings. (*She crosses to the telephone*) Good now that's settled, I'll ring the hospital and tell them to collect.

Julia You'll do nothing of the sort, Liz. You'll stop bloody well interfering in my affairs.

Liz But I have a legal duty—

Julia Sod your legal duty. Just go home and mind your own damn business. I don't want to see you ever again!

Liz Julia, you really are the most ungrateful cow.

Alex (*intervening*) It's all right Liz. I'll take over now.

Liz shrugs and crosses to exit

Liz (*to Alex as she passes*) I'll pop in tomorrow when she's quietened down. Try and get her to rest, dear ... give her a pill or something. 'Bye darling ...

She exits

Alex smiles a goodbye, then looks across at Julia

Alex You really must try and relax, Mother.

Julia (*finally taking a grip on herself*) I'm sorry ... it's all been a bit fraught.

Alex Yes, I'm sure. But don't worry. I'm here now. I'll sort it all out.

Julia (*quickly*) No need. Everything's under control.

Alex (*taking her by the arm*) Good. Now sit down and tell me all about it.

Julia sits down on the sofa

Julia There really isn't much to tell ...

Alex That must be the understatement of the week, Liz tells me you now have a lover.

Julia Yes ... we ... I was going to tell you about that later.

Alex You certainly didn't waste much time after Daddy left, did you?

Julia Did she also tell you that she was your father's mistress?

Alex Oh, I guessed that anyway.

Julia Then why didn't you tell me?

Alex It wasn't really my business.

Julia (*flaring up*) Then why are you being so bloody censorious about me taking a lover?

Alex That's different. Daddy loved women. With you it was just pique ... and a bit of middle-aged lust thrown in.

Julia Isn't it marvellous! Men can do as they like, but not women. We're supposed to remain faithful. Even after death.

Alex What do you mean "even after death"?

Julia Well, that's what you're implying.

Alex But you took your toy-boy before you knew that Daddy was dead. Didn't you, Mother? In fact, from your point of view, it was very convenient that he should die when he did.

Julia (*a beat*) What are you driving at?

Alex Just trying to establish the priorities in your mind. But let's move on to the point where, having drawn his pills, he came home to take them. When would that have been do you think? About what time?

Julia How should I know, I wasn't here.

Alex Of course, you were still in Paris with your stud.

Julia So what?

Alex You might have saved him. Given him heart massage, called an ambulance ... anything. You *might* have saved his life, Julia. Instead, you let him crawl upstairs to die like a wounded animal.

Julia No! I couldn't have saved him. It wouldn't have been possible.
Alex How do you know that?
Julia I refuse to be interrogated by my own daughter!
Alex Stepdaughter . . .
Julia I brought you up when your own mother walked out. Loved you, cared for you—
Alex (*stopping her*) Don't change the bloody subject!!!
Julia Alex, please . . . don't you think I've been through enough for the last few days? I've been torturing myself . . . thinking what I might have done . . . what I should not have done . . .
Alex All right, Julia. (*She gives a wan smile and crosses her fingers*) Pax?
Julia Oh, yes please . . .
Alex When I'm upset I feel I have to wound. I loved Daddy very much.
Julia Yes, I know darling.
Alex Mind if I play with your toy?
Julia Help yourself.

Alex crosses to the computer keyboard, looks it over professionally

Alex Nice micro. Aladdin Genie Mark Two six hundred and forty-K with polyphonic sound and modem attachment. Very versatile.
Julia You sound knowledgeable.
Alex We have them at college. I took a programming course.
Julia Really?
Alex My tutor seemed to think I was rather good at it.
Aladdin Hallo.
Alex (*keying and speaking*) Hallo.
Aladdin Would you like to play a game, Alex?
Alex (*keying "yes"*) What games have you got?
Aladdin Julia's game.
Julia I'm sure you don't want to play a game now.
Alex Yes I do. (*She keys in "?"*) I wonder what Julia's game is.
Julia Leave that damn thing alone.
Alex Why?
Julia Because it's evil!
Aladdin Murder.
Alex Computers aren't evil, Mother. They just do what evil people tell them.

Aladdin plays the "Dead March in Saul"

Now. Do we go through the whole program? Or may we take it as read.
Julia He said . . . he'd wiped that.
Alex Never trust a man who calls himself a high-technology specialist. Particularly Steven Jones. He was never all that hot.

Steven enters with a wreath

Steven They didn't have any forget-me-nots, so I went for lilies of the valley . . . (*He sees Alex*) Oh . . . hallo, poppet. How's tricks?
Aladdin The Murder Game. Who do you wish to murder, Alex?

Steven Oh ... there's a clever girl then.

Alex You can't wipe that memory, Steven. It's scored in a back-up chip and code-locked.

Steven You always were the brightest in the class.

Julia (*looking from one to the other*) You two know each other?

Steven (*with a smile*) Yes, you might say that.

Alex He was my tutor on the programming course. On loan from the Poly. He used to set us little exercises in code-breaking. Like how to rob the World Bank and give the proceeds to the Third World.

Steven That was a pushover.

Alex Or how to create the perfect murder.

Steven Bit more of a challenge that one.

Alex We had Susan Grey on our course. Her father's Jonathan Grey the specialist at the Mid-Anglia General. She gave us his personal entry code, and after that we were away.

Julia Alex, are you telling me you created the program that killed your father?

Alex It wasn't intended to kill anyone. It was just a game.

Julia And you gave it to him.

Alex No, he stole it.

Steven (*hurt*) Oh, come on ...

Alex Or perhaps, he just borrowed the computer with the Murder Game in its memory and never brought it back. The other night, thinking you might be feeling like a little company after Daddy had left I dropped in. I heard voices in your bedroom, yours, and his. So not wishing to play gooseberry, I went back to college. That night I began to think about it. (*Looking at Steven*) I knew Aladdin had the Murder Game and I knew what it could do. (*To Julia*) But I didn't think for one moment that you would go along with it. I thought you might act out some little fantasy, but not actually use it.

Julia I tried to call it off.

Alex (*talking over her*) The next morning I thought I'd check up, just in case. But another class were using the computers and I couldn't get access till just before ten ...

Julia We tried too, you must believe me ...

But Alex still talks over her, intent on her accusation

Alex When I finally got through, I found I was locked out. (*To Julia*) We were in deadly embrace you and I ... finally I broke through ...

Steven So you were the one who re-instated the decimal point.

Alex But I was too late. We were both too late. Daddy's appointment with the specialist was cancelled that morning, so he went straight to the dispensary to collect his pills.

Steven How did you know that?

Alex I called the hospital to find out.

Julia (*in alarm*) You rang the hospital?

Alex I tried to explain what happened, but they wouldn't believe me. After all, everything was back in place. They assumed I was a hoax caller and hung up ... Then I tried to get hold of Daddy ... I rang everywhere, but no-one knew where he was. I even rang here, but there was no answer ... not that it would have made any difference. By that time, he was almost certainly dead.

Steven So, what are you going to do? Call the police?

Alex They probably wouldn't believe me either. Where is the proof? It was the perfect murder. Even his doctor says it was accidental death ... You've got away with it.

Julia (*turning to Steven*) You planned it right from the start.

Steven No, I just led you to where you wanted to go, my lovely. And when you wanted to turn back, I went along with that too.

Julia When you first knocked on my door, you knew all about me. That my husband had just left me ... that he was heavily insured ... (*Turning to Alex*) And there's only one way you could have known that.

Steven Now that's the bit you've missed out amongst all your righteous indignation, isn't it, poppet. Our relationship.

Julia You came straight from her bed ... and into mine ... Oh God!

Steven Well, you were willing and eager. Like mother, like daughter, as they say.

Julia That's disgusting.

Steven There's nothing disgusting about it. I enjoyed you both. And I'm quite happy to go on with the same arrangement, if that's all right with you two.

Julia (*turning on Steven in fury*) Get out of my house!

Steven No. Nobody leaves. Nobody dare leave. We're all in this together. (*To Julia*) You and I may have committed the murder, if a murder was committed ... but Alex helped set up the program, even if she claims it was all done in innocence. We're all fellow conspirators. All in deadly embrace. And so long as we stick together no-one will ever know what happened. (*He crosses towards Aladdin*) Except you, Aladdin. And I'll have that program out of your memory bank if I have to smash every little chip in your busy little brain.

Alex You're too late, Steven, it's gone.

Steven What do you mean, gone?

Alex The genie's out of the bottle. Don't forget I've had that murder game ever since it was first set up at college. Do you think I didn't keep a copy? It's safely in my bank.

Steven (*after a fraction's pause*) What do you intend to do with it?

Alex That's my business. Maybe I'll just hold it over your head for the rest of your life like the sword of Damocles. Whatever I do, you have nothing to gain by hanging around here. If you think you're going to get a penny out of that quarter of a million my father left, you must be out of your tiny mind. Right, Mother?

Julia Right, Alex ...

Alex crosses upstage and opens the front door

Alex Goodbye, Steven Jones. Slip out the way you came and keep on running. Don't ever fall ill, whatever you do. Because I'll be watching you.

Steven Why did I ever get involved with male-friendly females? I should have stayed a five-inch floppy.

Steven exits through the front door

A moment's pause. Alex breaks the silence—she seems quite friendly, as if all was forgiven

Alex Are you all right, Mother?

Julia Bit shaky.

Alex Do you want one of your tablets?

Julia Thank you, Alex.

Alex Can I have a vodka?

Julia Of course, darling help yourself.

Alex Do you want one?

Julia I shouldn't really with those pills, but I suppose a small one won't hurt. (*After a pause, still uncertain of how Alex is going to behave*) I still find it hard to believe that any of this ever happened.

Alex Yes . . .

Julia When I think of how he must have been planning this for weeks—months . . . taking advantage of the fact that I felt abandoned.

Alex brings the vodka and pill

Thank you, dear. (*She takes the pill*)

Alex It takes two to tango, Mother.

Julia Oh yes . . . I'm not saying I wasn't part of it or anything . . . but . . .

Alex Only a small and reluctant part.

Julia I—er—haven't been feeling very well lately. Hypertension the doctor says. Not that he's any use. All they ever do these days is dish you out with pills, pills and more pills until in the end you don't know what you're taking.

Alex looks at her. Another pause

I think your father really did die of a heart attack, you know.

Alex Really?

Julia The doctor was absolutely convinced. And he should know, shouldn't he?

Alex Yes.

Julia I think I'll have another drink.

Alex Yes.

Julia I'm not saying that I won't feel desperately guilty for the rest of my life.

Alex (*still quite calm, showing no emotion*) Oh, I'm sure you'll get over it. (*Suddenly changing the subject, she settles down on a chair as though for a chat, facing her mother and watching her every reaction*) I had to take a seminar the other week, for my group. Looking back now, it was almost prophetic.

Julia Yes?

Alex We were discussing the increasing role of the computer in decision-making. Not just practical decisions but even, now, moral decisions.

Julia I'd rather you didn't talk about that damn thing if you don't mind.

Alex I thought you might like to know what we discuss at college. We never really talk about it.

Julia Yes, of course. It's just that I'm not feeling very well ...

Alex Justice outside the law. Far more inexorable than anything administered by people, because there is no room for error or compassion.

Julia Alex ... I'm ... feeling ... very ... ill.

Alex You see the trouble is, you're trying to pretend it never happened. But it did happen, Julia. You murdered my father. And for that you deserve to die.

Julia Uh? (*She sinks to her knees*)

Alex I said you deserve to die, Julia ... and you are going to die. You are dying now, at this very moment.

Julia is by now unintelligible

Two can play computer games Julia ... Chlorpromazine. It's a very powerful relaxant. But ten times the normal dose would be fatal.

Julia is now quite still

It's only a matter of moments now, Mother dear. I've never really liked you, Julia ... you tried but things just weren't the same after Mummy left ... but I did love Daddy. You see I loved my father very much.

Alex goes to the computer, keys in

Game over.

Aladdin Who next?

Alex Steven Jones.

Aladdin Age of victim.

Steven enters the front door and moves towards Alex's chair

Alex Thirty-five.

Aladdin Sex.

Alex Male.

Aladdin Motive. Select from: One: money. Two: jealousy. Three: revenge ...

As Alex turns round ...

Black-out

CURTAIN

FURNITURE AND PROPERTY LIST

ACT I

Scene 1

On stage: Sitting-room area:
Bookshelves overflowing with books
Sofa
Coffee table. *On it:* papers, books
2 spoonbacked chairs
Rocking chair
Footstool
Victorian canterbury. *In it:* magazines, papers
Jardinière with maidenhair fern
Rolltop desk. *On it:* telephone, small computer, books, papers
Chairs
Round table. *On it:* bills, credit card statements, papers, books, desk diary
Marble fireplace. *Above it:* gilt mirror
Mantelpiece. *On it:* pieces of fine china, old shells, fossils
Drinks cupboard. *In it:* bottles of drink including vodka, glasses. *On top:* pile of papers
Chest. *In it:* papers
Persian carpet
Peruvian scatter mats
On walls: good prints, art deco posters, "Save the Whale" poster
Window curtains
Bin bag
Hoover plugged into wall socket
Doormat

Kitchen area:
Sink unit with practical taps
Cooker
Kitchen units. *On one:* percolator, kettle, coffee. *In cupboards:* cups, saucers, etc., glasses, cutlery
Fridge/freezer. *In freezer compartment:* trays of ice

Gallery area:
Double bed with pillows, duvet, sheet
Man's pyjamas under pillow
Bedside table. *On it:* lamp

Off stage: Man's dressing-gown, hairbrush, toothbrush **(Julia)**
Weekend bag **(Alex)**
Pyjama trousers **(Liz)**

Personal: **Julia:** handkerchief
Liz: handbag

SCENE 2

Strike: Pyjama trousers

Re-set: Front door open

Off stage: Briefcase containing clipboard, 5-inch floppy disc, 8-inch hard disc,
              package of floppy discs, manual; large cardboard box containing
              cases with large computer, elaborate keyboard, VDU, printer,
              modem **(Steven)**

Personal: **Steven:** business card

SCENE 3

Set: **Julia**'s clothing and shoes by bed
              Steven's shoes, socks, jacket by bed

Re-set: Telephone receiver back on telephone

Off stage: Holdall with pants, toothbrush **(Steven)**

ACT II

SCENE 1

Strike: Hoover
              Clothing, shoes, etc. from gallery
              Holdall
              Cardboard boxes

Re-set: Telephone receiver back on telephone
              Tidy room

Set: Packet of photographs

Off stage: Bunch of flowers **(Steven)**

Personal: **Julia:** wrist-watch

SCENE 2

Strike: Bunch of flowers
              Photographs

Re-set: Telephone receiver back on telephone
              Duvet concealing body on bed

Set: Letters, two copies of the *Cambridge News* on doormat

Off stage: Small suitcase, handbag with £10 note **(Julia)**
              Larger suitcase **(Steven)**
              Small bag, envelope containing ear-ring **(Receptionist)**
              Bottle of vodka **(Steven)**

Strike:	Dirty glasses
	Suitcases
	Small bag, envelope, ear-ring
	New bottle of vodka
	Letters, newspapers

Re-set: Bed made up properly

Set: Bottle of pills on drinks cabinet

Off stage: Carrier bag, handbag containing will **(Liz)**
Wreath **(Steven)**

Personal: **Steven:** wrist-watch

LIGHTING PLOT

Practical fittings required: wall brackets in living area and bedroom gallery, bedside lamp

Interior. A sitting-room with gallery bedroom and kitchen area

ACT I, SCENE 1   Morning

To open: Black-out

Cue 1	When ready	(Page 1)
	Bring up general lighting	
Cue 2	**Julia:** ". . . to kill the bastard!"	(Page 6)
	Fade to Black-out	

ACT I, SCENE 2   Late afternoon

To open: General lighting, beginning to fade

Cue 3	**Julia** keys in her name on computer	(Page 10)
	Eerie halo of light around computer	
Cue 4	**Steven** and **Julia** go into tight clinch	(Page 13)
	Begin to fade lights	
Cue 5	**Steven** and **Julia** settle on bed	(Page 13)
	Fade to Black-out	

ACT I, SCENE 3   Evening

To open: Dim lighting

Cue 6	**Julia** switches on bedside lamp	(Page 13)
	Snap up bedside lamp	
Cue 7	**Steven** switches on main lights	(Page 13)
	Snap up wall-brackets and general lighting downstairs	
Cue 8	**Julia:** "H.A.L.L.O. Enter." (*She presses button on computer*)	(Page 14)
	Eerie halo of light round computer	
Cue 9	**Steven:** ". . . it's only a game."	(Page 22)
	Begin to fade lights	
Cue 10	**Julia:** "Only a game . . ."	(Page 22)
	Fade to Black-out	

ACT II, SCENE 1   Morning

To open: General lighting; eerie halo of light round computer

Cue 11   **Steven:** "... while we're away. Huh?"   (Page 29)
             Fade to Black-out

ACT II, SCENE 2   Day

To open: General lighting

Cue 12   **Liz** switches on bedroom lights   (Page 37)
             Snap up wall-brackets in bedroom

Cue 13   **Julia:** "Michael ... Michael ..."   (Page 37)
             Black-out

ACT II, SCENE 3   Day

To open: General lighting; eerie glow of light round computer

Cue 14   As **Alex** turns round   (Page 46)
             Black-out

EFFECTS PLOT

ACT I

Cue 1   Before Lights come up   (Page 1)
Chatter of electronic sound signals from computer, gradually forming recognizable tune—opening bars to the "Dead March in Saul"—fade as **Julia** *enters*

Cue 2   Shortly after Scene 2 begins   (Page 6)
Van approaches, pulls up outside on gravel, engine is turned off, door slams

Cue 3   **Julia** keys in her name   (Page 10)
Mad squeaking noise from computer which forms itself into recognizable "good-morning" tune

Cue 4   **Steven** (*off*): "... press 'enter'."   (Page 14)
Shower, off

Cue 5   **Julia:** "H.A.L.L.O. Enter." (*She presses a button*)   (Page 14)
Squeaking noise from computer, then "good-morning" tune

Cue 6   **Julia:** "... you idiot machine!"   (Page 15)
Telephone rings

Cue 7   **Steven** (*off*) "Press 'exit'."   (Page 15)
Shower stops

Cue 8   **Julia** presses button on computer   (Page 15)
Squeak from computer

Cue 9   **Steven:** "All right. Press three." **Julia** *keys in*   (Page 16)
Computer plays first few bars of "Dead March in Saul"

Cue 10   **Aladdin:** "Wait please."   (Page 19)
Dialling sound

Cue 11   **Steven:** "That's the incredible thing." *They wait*   (Page 20)
After a moment, squeaking from computer

Cue 12   **Aladdin:** "Line now clear."   (Page 20)
Computer plays "Pop Goes the Weasel" on synthesizer

ACT II

Cue 13   **Steven:** "Look, he's on great form."   (Page 22)
Repeat Cue 12

Cue 14   **Steven** starts to key instructions   (Page 25)
Whirring, squeaking sound from computer as it goes through its code strings

MADE AND PRINTED IN GREAT BRITAIN BY
LATIMER TREND & COMPANY LTD PLYMOUTH

MADE IN ENGLAND